WORLD WAR II WEAPONS

WORLD WAR II WEAPONS

ESSENTIAL LIBRARY OF
★ WORLD ★
WAR II

Essential Library

An Imprint of Abdo Publishing
abdopublishing.com

BY ARNOLD RINGSTAD

CONTENT CONSULTANT

JAMES D. SCUDIERI, PHD
RESEARCH ANALYST
ARMY HERITAGE AND EDUCATION CENTER (AHEC), CARLISLE, PENNSYLVANIA

Published by Abdo Publishing, a division of ABDO, PO Box 398166, Minneapolis, Minnesota 55439. Copyright © 2016 by Abdo Consulting Group, Inc. International copyrights reserved in all countries. No part of this book may be reproduced in any form without written permission from the publisher. Essential Library™ is a trademark and logo of Abdo Publishing.

Printed in the United States of America, North Mankato, Minnesota

052015
092015

Cover Photos: AP Images
Interior Photos: AP Images, 1, 3, 6, 8, 16, 23, 26, 31, 36, 39, 48, 51, 53, 63, 66, 78, 83, 86, 88, 91, 97, 98 (top), 98 (bottom), 99 (bottom); Berliner Verlag/Archiv/Picture-Alliance/DPA/AP Images, 11, 47, 58; PFC Phillip Scheer/US Marine Corp History Division, 15; ClassicStock/Corbis, 20; Shutterstock Images, 25, 43; Public Domain, 29; US Army Signal Corps, 34; Archiv Neumann/Picture-Alliance/DPA/AP Images, 44; Ordnance Corps Training and Heritage Center, Fort Lee, VA, 55; Bettmann/Corbis, 60, 68, 76, 99 (top); US Navy/AP Images, 73, 75; Hulton-Deutsch Collection/Corbis, 81; Picture-Alliance/DPA/AP Images, 93

Editor: Karen Latchana Kenney
Series Designers: Kelsey Oseid and Maggie Villaume

Library of Congress Control Number: 2015931118

Cataloging-in-Publication Data

Ringstad, Arnold.
 World War II weapons / Arnold Ringstad.
   p. cm. -- (Essential library of World War II)
Includes bibliographical references and index.
ISBN 978-1-62403-799-3
1. Military weapons--History--20th century--Juvenile literature. 2. World War, 1939-1945--Equipment and supplies--Juvenile literature. I. Title.

CONTENTS

German Ju 87 dive bombers in formation, 1940

WAGING A NEW WAR

On September 1, 1939, hundreds of German Ju 87 dive bombers flew over the Polish border, symbolic of a new, powerful German air force. Clearing the path for a German invasion of Poland, they were striking some of the first blows of World War II (1939–1945). Groups of the two-man single-winged aircraft, nicknamed the Stuka, began a relentless assault on Poland's military, infrastructure, and people. Pilots flew high to locate targets and then took steep vertical dives toward them. Air brakes slowed their descent and allowed pilots to zero in on the targets. Vertical dive-bombing was up to four times as accurate as dropping bombs while flying level.

Wind-powered sirens attached to each plane's landing gear generated a distinctive howling noise designed to terrify those on

A Polish train lays destroyed after a German attack in 1939.

the ground. At the last possible moment, the pilots released the bombs, flung by a trapeze-like arm to avoid hitting the aircraft's propeller.

Each carrying more than 1,000 pounds (450 kg) of bombs, the Stukas struck Polish army units, bridges, railways, airfields, and lines of communication.[1] Their objective was to paralyze Polish defenses and clear the way for masses of German tanks, motorized infantry, and artillery crossing the border from three directions. The bulk of the German infantry followed on foot. Accompanied by infantry on trucks and motorized artillery, the armor quickly smashed through the Polish frontline forces and reached deep into Poland. Rampaging across Poland over the next several weeks, German forces encircled large pockets of Polish troops. The Russians invaded Poland from the east two weeks later. The entire campaign lasted approximately five weeks.

Poland had been subjected to a new type of war, far different from the protracted stalemate of World War I (1914–1918). As he watched a teacher lead a group of students toward trees for shelter, Polish military officer Wladyslaw Anders described a scene he witnessed that suggested this war would be a brutal one:

> *Suddenly there was the roar of an aeroplane. The pilot circled, descending to a height of fifty meters. As he dropped his bombs and fired his machine-guns, the children scattered like sparrows. The aeroplane disappeared as quickly as it had come, but on the field some crumpled and lifeless bundles of bright clothing remained. The nature of the new war was already clear.*[2]

GERMANY VERSUS POLAND

At the dawn of World War II, Germany possessed enormous advantages over Poland. The German army contained 2.5 million troops, while Poland had 280,000 troops. The German air force had approximately 3,600 aircraft, while Poland had barely half as many.[3] Additionally, Poland's most important areas were close to German-controlled territory, which bordered Poland on three sides. A rapid German strike ensured that these areas fell quickly. Germany also had economic advantages. The annual budget of Berlin, Germany's capital city, was greater than that of the entire nation of Poland.

BLITZKRIEG WARFARE

Anders was seeing the rehearsal for the German blitzkrieg, or "lightning war." In this new style of warfare, coordinated aircraft, tanks, and mechanized and motorized units provided rapid, overwhelming firepower against the enemy's frontline forces. The speed of their movement left enemy defenses confused and unable to organize counterattacks. The Germans' ability to strike swiftly and deeply into the heart of enemy territory meant armies could avoid the deadlock of the World War I trenches. This conflict was also a total war, involving civilian populations as never before.

Behind the rapid advance, supply and communication lines were set up to enable the invading forces to continue pushing forward, but the swiftly advancing armored forces would not wait. At the same time, propaganda campaigns attacked enemy morale. The goal was to quickly eliminate the enemy's ability and will to resist. The evolution of blitzkrieg was possible because of Germany's military buildup during the 1930s and its highly developed organization and coordination of its forces.

Blitzkrieg proved extremely effective in the early months of World War II. After crushing Poland, Germany turned its attention to France. In the spring of 1940, Germany used blitzkrieg to seize France in a matter of weeks. German leader Adolf Hitler then turned his attention to the United Kingdom. But in the summer of 1940, the Stuka proved extremely vulnerable to modern British fighter planes. The Stukas were withdrawn from the Battle of Britain.

More limitations of German blitzkrieg were revealed when Germany invaded the Soviet Union in the summer of 1941, drawing the Soviets into the war.

A Nazi banner reads "German villages in Danzig land keep a faithful watch on the banks of the Weichsel," hinting at their upcoming invasion of the town in 1939.

The initial thrusts into the vast Soviet frontier succeeded greatly. However, German forces, most of which relied on horses, were unable to maintain supply lines. The new war spanned an area many times the size of earlier conquests in France. By winter, the cold weather stopped German advances. When the Soviets began large-scale counterattacks, they had established deep defenses that could absorb the German blitzkrieg-style attacks.

STUKA ACE

In the hands of a skilled pilot, the Stuka could make a devastating difference on the battlefield. Germany's top Stuka pilot of the war was Hans-Ulrich Rudel. In a specialized Stuka designed for antitank missions, Rudel flew combat missions against the Soviet Union on the eastern front. At sea, he destroyed a battleship, a cruiser, and a destroyer. But most of his flying was done over land, where he destroyed 519 Soviet tanks.[4]

BUILDING TOWARD WAR

By the late summer of 1939, leaders of the world's great powers knew war was coming. In Germany, Hitler and his Nazi Party were in total control of the nation and its military. Hitler had seized territory near Germany without firing a shot, including Austria in 1938 and Czechoslovakia in 1939. In Africa, the armed forces of Italian Fascist dictator Benito Mussolini had conquered Ethiopia by 1936. Halfway around the world, the Empire of Japan was expanding its territory on mainland Asia into China. The three nations, known together as the Axis powers, consolidated their gains, built up their militaries, and planned further conquests.

Japan and Germany prioritized modernizing their armed forces, subordinating other domestic efforts. International treaties signed following

Germany's loss in World War I had limited the size and capabilities of Germany's military. After Hitler took power in 1933, the country began rearming openly during the 1930s. It constructed modern tanks, planes, and other weapons. Other treaties limited the size and power of Japan's navy. Defying these agreements in 1936, Japan began building an enormous and powerful navy. It would allow them to contest US power in the Pacific Ocean.

The world's other great powers included the United Kingdom, France, the Soviet Union, and the United States. They would eventually be known as the Allied powers. At first, these countries did little to respond to these territorial and military advances. Some of Hitler's land gains had come through political agreements with the United Kingdom and France, rather than conquest. But after Germany's invasion of Poland, the United Kingdom and France finally felt compelled to act. On September 3, 1939, they declared war on Germany. In the summer of 1941, a German invasion of the Soviet Union led the Soviets to align themselves with the British. In December of that year, Japan attacked Pearl Harbor, a US military base in Hawaii. The United States immediately declared war on Japan. As Japan's ally, Germany responded by declaring war on the United States. By the end of 1941, all the major world powers were involved in the conflict.

MAKING WAR

For many people, weapons defined World War II. They were what made the war possible. But just as important as weapons were the abilities to design, build, and use them. The outcome of the war was ultimately determined not only by technological achievements, but also by economic superiority. Throughout the war, less powerful weapons often emerged victorious through sheer force of numbers. This was a result of armies' and their soldiers' abilities to adapt to wartime conditions and find innovative uses for the weapons they had.

Germany's later advanced tank designs could not stand up to the massive waves of tanks built and deployed by the Soviet Union, the United States, and the United Kingdom, especially given issues with the reliability of German machines that emerged through the war. Further, US production capacity proved a decisive factor in the war. The country was willing and able to spend vast sums of money building its military to fight and win a long war. US General George S. Patton remarked:

> Americans as a race are the most adept in the use of machinery of any people on earth, and . . . the most adept in the construction of machines on a mass-production basis. It costs about $40,000 for a man to get killed. If we can keep him from being killed by a few extra dollars, it is a cheap expenditure.[5]

The United States was willing to use all of its industrial might, involving all of its society. It ordered the production of a total of 296,000 aircraft and 86,333 tanks during World War II.[6] After relocating its industrial facilities far behind the front lines after the German invasion, the Soviet Union kept its weapon production lines running high as well. The nation manufactured nearly 15 million rifles and carbines during the course of the conflict.[7] The United States also provided billions of dollars in aid to its allies, especially the Soviet Union and the United Kingdom, under the Lend-Lease program.

Rugged weapon and equipment designs were key in challenging conditions such as mud.

The Allied weapons of World War II were not necessarily the most powerful or technologically advanced. The ability of the Allies to build balanced, effective weapons in large numbers was critical. Complex, advanced weapons worked well in theory. But in the dusty, muddy, grimy reality of war, simple and rugged designs often proved more reliable. The most successful weapons of the war struck a balance between these critical factors.

Many people made it possible to develop and produce these weapons. Academic researchers at universities studied the basic principles of new technology. Workers in the weapons industries designed and built weapons that took advantage of these principles. Government officials made the final decisions to use these weapons in battle.

German infantry march through Prague, Czechoslovakia, on March 19, 1939.

SMALL ARMS

In the 1900s, countries began waging war with more advanced technology. Modern weapons of World War II ranged from high-flying bombers to lumbering tanks and stealthy submarines. But some of the most important weapons of the war were also the simplest—the rifles the infantry carried.

The basic role of the infantry is to capture enemy territory on foot, then defend that ground. Small arms, which are light weapons easily carried and fired by a single soldier, are key to carrying out the infantry role. Early in World War II, as the Germans attacked Poland and France, tanks appeared able to take the place of infantry in land warfare. However, infantry soldiers soon showed they were as important as ever. Battles demonstrated how victory depended on the cooperation of all parts of an army, especially in cities, jungles, and mountains where the tanks could not go. Portable antitank weapons allowed individual soldiers to defeat heavily armored tanks.

The role of infantry remained essentially the same, but the weapons they carried changed significantly over the course of the war. In 1939, most soldiers carried the same weapons that had been used in World War I, more than two decades earlier. These were typically bolt-action rifles. With these weapons, a soldier could fire only a single shot before having to manually load the next round. The result was a slow rate of fire. The bolt-action rifles of World War II included the British Lee-Enfield, the German Mauser, and the Soviet Mosin-Nagant.

While most nations continued using bolt-action rifles as their standard weapons during World War II, advances implemented during the war changed infantry weapons forever. The US military introduced the first widespread semiautomatic rifle, the M1. This design automatically loaded the next round after firing. It dramatically increased the amount of firepower each soldier could generate. Another key development came from Germany. A new type of weapon

BRUTAL WARFARE

Infantry combat was brutally violent, especially in the Pacific, where Japanese troops frequently charged Allied positions. US Marine Corps Corporal Alvy Ray Pittman recalled a particularly horrifying example of this brutality:

A [Japanese soldier] jumped up and grabbed one of our men. What the enemy would do is grab someone and hit his grenade on his own helmet [to trigger it] and then hold the grenade between them so they would both be killed. The marine grabbed the [Japanese soldier], pinning his arms so he could not start the fuse of the grenade. And they were dancing around, and somebody else went up and shot the [Japanese soldier] in the head with a forty-five.[1]

known as the assault rifle put even more firepower into the hands of individual soldiers. It would continue firing automatically as long as the trigger was being pulled. The Germans produced it too late to affect the war. However, after the war, assault rifles soon became standard equipment for infantry all over the world.

A WAR-WINNING RIFLE

The official name of the M1 rifle was the Rifle, Caliber .30, M1. But it was best known as the Garand. Canadian gun designer John C. Garand designed this weapon more than a decade before the start of World War II. The US military officially accepted it in 1932, making it the first semiautomatic rifle in the US arsenal.

The Garand was an extraordinarily well-designed weapon. It was expensive and complex to manufacture compared with earlier bolt-action types. However, the US military buildup in the years leading up to the war meant that by the time the country entered World War II in 1941, most US forces were equipped with the Garand.

Following the United States' entrance into the war, the speed at which new troops joined the US military outpaced the speed at which Garands could be produced. New recruits were often equipped with outdated rifles, while factories accelerated their production of the complicated semiautomatic weapons. US production capacity eventually caught up. By the end of the war, the United States had produced approximately 5.5 million Garands.[2]

The Garand was a popular and versatile weapon. With normal use, it fired a 0.3-inch (7.62 mm) round. This measurement, known as a weapon's caliber,

US Army infantry shoot their M1 rifles while in action on March 1, 1944.

indicates the diameter of the bullets the weapon fires. Users lined up their shots through iron sights on the weapon. A telescopic sight could be added, allowing snipers to make long-range shots. In 1943, a grenade launcher attachment was introduced. Soldiers could use it to shoot grenades many times farther than they could throw them.

Despite its effectiveness, the Garand had a few notable downsides. First, the reloading system was awkward. The Garand used clips containing eight bullets, giving a soldier eight shots before he had to reload. But it was only possible to reload using a full eight-round clip. Additionally, when the eighth bullet fired, the weapon automatically ejected the empty clip with a loud "ping" sound. This could alert nearby enemy forces that a soldier had an empty rifle.

Overall, the Garand was met with high praise. US general George S. Patton described it as "the greatest battle implement ever devised."[3] Even the Axis nations respected the Garand. When German forces captured the rifles on the battlefield, they put them into service under the name Selbstladegewehr 251(a), or "self-loading rifle."

THE BIRTH OF THE ASSAULT RIFLE

In the age of bolt-action weapons, an army's rifle-carrying infantry typically went into battle along with machine gunners who provided rapid-firing power. A new weapon changed this battle tactic forever. The German military introduced the Sturmgewehr assault rifle in 1943. These weapons sprayed large-caliber bullets at a rapid pace, multiplying the firepower an individual soldier could bring to the battlefield.

Assault rifles were not the first handheld automatic weapons. While mired in World War I, warring nations found a need for portable automatic weapons that could quickly clear enemy trenches. Submachine guns filled this need. The US Thompson submachine gun and the German MP38 are both World War II examples of this type. Submachine guns fired at a rapid rate, but they used the same size ammunition typically used in pistols. As a result, the submachine guns were useful only at short range and lacked the sheer stopping power of rifle ammunition.

TOMMY GUNS

The Thompson submachine gun was designed during World War I, but the finished guns were not ready before the war ended in 1918. Rather than gaining fame on the battlefield, the weapons—nicknamed tommy guns—were widely used by gangs in the United States during the 1920s. Prohibition, a ban on the sale of alcoholic beverages, was in effect, and gangs became active in the illegal market for alcohol. This led to violent confrontations with police, in which gangsters sometimes wielded tommy guns. The link with crime was solidified by the gun's appearance in Hollywood gangster movies. It was not until 1938 that the military began purchasing the Thompson in large numbers.

The Sturmgewehr 44, however, fired larger 0.31-inch (7.92 mm) rounds, even bigger in diameter than the rounds fired by the M1 Garand. But firepower is determined not only by a round's diameter, but also by the amount of propellant launching the round forward. The more propellant there is, the faster the bullet travels. More propellant also means more recoil—the amount of force pushing back on the weapon's user while firing.

Using a rifle-sized round in a fully automatic rifle would result in massive recoil, making it difficult to aim the weapon. As a compromise, the designers of the Sturmgewehr 44 reduced the amount of propellant in each round. This cut down on recoil while still making the weapon more powerful than a submachine gun. The Germans also slowed the rate of fire to assist with accuracy. With these innovations, the assault rifle was born. The basic design is still standard in militaries around the world today.

PISTOLS

By the time of World War II, pistols were in many ways obsolete. Carbines filled pistols' roles. These weapons can be held in one hand, making them easier to

US soldiers assemble Thompson submachine guns in a small arms shop in England on January 27, 1943.

handle in confined spaces. Pistols lacked both accuracy and range. Despite these downsides, pistols remained popular among soldiers. Many treasured their pistols, and some even took pistols from fallen enemies as trophies.

One of the best-known pistols of World War II, the German Luger, was introduced in 1908. It remained in production through 1942. The weapon had a complex design, but it was reliable in combat. As the German economy worked to produce a vast array of weapons, its military decided the Luger was no longer worth the time and resources it cost to build. Allied soldiers often collected the iconic, rugged Luger pistols as troops fought across Europe.

Similar to the Luger, the most important US pistol of World War II was invented before World War I. The Colt M1911, named for the year it was accepted into US military service, fired a large 0.4-inch (11 mm) round. Its designers sought more stopping power than was provided by older 0.38-inch (9.7 mm) ammunition.

THE LIBERATOR PISTOL

One of the war's most unusual weapons was the American FP-45 pistol, known as the Liberator. This tiny pistol was capable of holding just one bullet. Designed for cheap, simple mass production and use by resistance fighters in occupied nations, it was intended to be airdropped into enemy territory. The United States dropped the weapons over Europe and shipped them to China, but in smaller numbers than imagined. The Liberator came packed in a plastic bag, along with ten 0.4-inch (11 mm) bullets and cartoon pictures that explained how to use the gun. The United States built approximately 1 million Liberator pistols, but there are no reliable records of how many were actually distributed or how people in occupied areas used them.[4]

A German Luger pistol, helmet, and Iron Cross medal from World War II

Canadian soldiers stationed in England practiced with a twin-barreled Browning machine gun on April 22, 1941.

CHAPTER
★ 3 ★

HEAVY WEAPONS

Rifles, submachine guns, and assault rifles were the primary weapons of most soldiers who fought during World War II. However, forces on all sides often encountered tasks for which these weapons were completely inadequate. Laying down rapid, long-duration supporting fire, assaulting fortified bunkers, and destroying enemy tanks all required specialized weapons operated by trained soldiers. To accomplish these missions, soldiers used large machine guns, flamethrowers, and antitank weapons.

MACHINE GUNS

Unlike smaller submachine guns and assault rifles, full-size machine guns are too large and unwieldy for a single moving soldier to use. Instead these guns are used from stationary positions, stabilized by a bipod or tripod. Light machine guns and general-purpose machine guns were typically supported on a bipod and could be moved around relatively easily. Heavy machine guns often used a tripod, were more unwieldy, and were more powerful. Machine guns became infamous for their killing power during the static trench warfare of World War I. Troops mostly remained in their side's trenches, launching assaults from there on enemy trenches. During these charges, a few defensive machine gunners could cut down dozens of attackers. The battles of World War II were typically much more mobile, lacking the large-scale charges of World War I. But machine guns still generated enough firepower to force enemy troops behind cover.

The German MG 42 general-purpose machine gun did not enter combat until 1942, but it quickly became one of the most effective large machine guns of the war. It went on to be used against the Allies on every front. In addition to its combat capability, it also became notable for its innovative production. Its designers created it with a streamlined production process in mind, making it easier for the Germans to build a large number of the guns quickly and cheaply.

As German forces withdrew to the borders of Germany in 1944, outnumbered by the United States and the United Kingdom to the west and the Soviet Union to the east, the MG 42 proved to be a valuable defensive tool. The machine

TRACER ROUNDS

Machine guns and other weapons are sometimes equipped with tracer rounds. These bullets produce a visible trail of light when fired. Mixing in tracer rounds with normal bullets can help gunners correct their aim. German MG 42 crews used tracers to their advantage. One gunner, using tracer rounds, would fire well above the heads of Allied troops. If the troops stood up and exposed themselves after seeing the wrongly aimed tracer fire, a second MG 42 would open fire with normal ammunition.

JOHN BROWNING
1855–1926

One of the most influential designers of guns used in World War II died in 1926, more than a decade before the war began. American gun designer John Browning was born in Utah in 1855. At age 24, he patented his first gun—a rifle. He later experimented with shotguns and machine guns. Browning eventually developed several weapons used by the United States in World War II. They include the M1911 pistol, the Browning Automatic Rifle (BAR), and the M2 machine gun.

Browning focused on increasing the reliability and rate of fire of his weapons. In the 1880s, he began developing a weapon that would fire automatically, without the user needing to operate a lever or pump to fire the next shot. Browning noticed that guns expelled gases from their muzzles when fired. He developed mechanisms that put the energy from these gases to work loading the next round. Further development of this idea led to the BAR and the M2 0.5 inch (12.7 mm).

gun had an extremely high rate of fire, ideally capable of shooting up to 1,550 rounds per minute.[1] This made it possible for a small number of troops to have a significant effect on advancing enemy forces. However, such a high rate of fire also caused the gun's barrel to quickly overheat, requiring the MG 42's designers to incorporate a system for quickly changing barrels.

Another highly successful machine gun was the US Browning M2 heavy machine gun. Firing a large 0.5-inch (12.7 mm) round, the M2 was extremely powerful and versatile. It was mounted on heavy vehicles, such as tanks and armored cars, and it could be equipped with armor-piercing ammunition to attack enemy vehicles. The gun attached to tripods for use against infantry. Multiple M2s could be mounted together for defense against low-flying aircraft. This defense was used at sea on US Navy vessels and on land vehicles.

FLAMETHROWERS

Flamethrowers were among the war's most terrifying weapons. A flamethrower consisted of a backpack holding flammable fuel. It attached to a handheld gun that ignited and launched the fluid. Anyone hit by the flame died a gruesome and painful death. Simply the sight and sound of a flamethrower destroyed enemy morale. As a result, enemy troops typically targeted flamethrower troops as soon as they appeared. This made the flamethrower's job one of the most dangerous in the military. Still, the effectiveness of the weapon meant it remained in use until the war's end. When used against enemy bunkers, the flamethrower's fire consumed the oxygen in the enclosed space, suffocating enemy troops within.

The United States continued developing and revising its flamethrower arsenal throughout World War II. Its M1 flamethrower first saw combat in January 1943

A US Marine uses a flamethrower against a Japanese guard post.

at the Battle of Guadalcanal in the Pacific. Its users soon found severe faults with it, and it frequently failed to work properly. The revised M1A1, ready by June 1943, used a new fuel that gave the weapon longer range. Still, mechanical issues with the ignition system plagued the weapon. The next major version, the M2-2, featured a reworked ignition and proved much more reliable. It first saw combat with US troops in the Pacific in July 1944. Nearly 25,000 of these flamethrowers were produced before the war's end.[2]

Flamethrowers could clear out foxholes and bunkers, but US forces made extensive use of them in the Pacific for another specialized purpose. Anticipating US invasions, Japanese forces dug large networks of caves on many small islands dotting the Pacific. In addition to providing protection from naval bombardment, the cave systems made it possible to move troops and supplies from place to place. Clearing out these caves with normal infantry was a difficult task. Flamethrowers provided an alternate method. The fire produced by flamethrowers consumed the oxygen in enclosed caves. If caves were too large for this tactic, troops would sometimes resort to simply bulldozing the entrances shut.

FLAMETHROWERS AT IWO JIMA

The brutal Battle of Iwo Jima, fought between Japan and the United States in early 1945 on the Pacific island of Iwo Jima, saw heavy flamethrower use. Japanese troops on the island had built a vast network of caves, including many within Mount Suribachi, the peak that towers over the small island's southern end. Corporal Herschel Williams of the US Marine Corps was awarded the Medal of Honor, the highest US military award, for his actions with a flamethrower at Iwo Jima.

His Medal of Honor citation describes the event, emphasizing the power of the weapon:

On one occasion he daringly mounted a pillbox to insert the nozzle of his flame thrower through the air vent, kill the occupants and silence the gun; on another he grimly charged enemy riflemen who attempted to stop him with bayonets and destroyed them with a burst of flame from his weapon.[3]

Because flamethrower troops were quickly targeted, armies took special steps to protect them. Rifle-carrying troops protected US flamethrowers. The Soviet Union used a different strategy. They disguised the gun portion of their flamethrowers to resemble rifles, and the fuel tank on the back was disguised as an ordinary backpack. This made it more difficult for enemy troops to identify the flamethrowers.

DESTROYING TANKS

The rapid technological developments in the 1920s and 1930s and the dramatic successes of Hitler's attacks on Poland and France made it clear tanks would play an important role in the war. Equipped with large cannons, machine guns, and thick armor, they presented an intimidating appearance to infantry armed only with rifles. Warring nations soon realized they needed a way for infantry to counter tanks. One of the most successful classes of weapons was the antitank rocket, after antitank rifles proved disappointing and inadequate.

The most famous of these antitank weapons was the US bazooka. The weapon's development began in early 1942, and bazookas saw combat in North Africa before the end of the year. The bazooka was simple yet effective. It was a steel tube that was open at both ends. The rocket left through the forward end, while its exhaust flew out through the back end. Two-man crews operated bazookas—one aimed and fired the weapon, while the other loaded rockets.

The explosives at the tip of the bazooka's 2.36-inch (6 cm) diameter rockets were key to its success.[4] Ordinary explosives would bounce off the thick armor, but a new development known as the shaped charge focused the rocket's explosive into a smaller area to blast through thick armor. In addition to being

A US soldier holds a bazooka, one antitank weapon used during the war.

used against tanks, troops also used bazookas to attack enemy bunkers, clear barbed wire obstacles, and even blast paths through minefields. The United States built more than 450,000 bazookas over the course of the war.[5]

Early German antitank weapons were less sophisticated. In late 1943, German troops began using the Panzerfaust, a simple rocket-propelled grenade launcher with a shaped charge. It was a single-shot weapon, and its range was short, sometimes as little as 98 feet (30 m).[6]

When Allied and German forces struggled for control of Tunisia in North Africa in early 1943, some US bazookas fell into the hands of the Axis powers. German engineers were impressed with the design and set to work developing a copy. The result was the Panzerschreck. Like the bazooka, it was a hollow tube open at both ends. Its designers used a larger rocket than was used in the bazooka, making it deadly against most Allied tanks.

SOVIET DOG MINES

Some Soviet forces adopted desperate weapons in an attempt to counter the threat posed by German tanks. One such weapon was the dog mine. Soviet dog handlers trained dogs to dive beneath enemy tanks. In battle, the dogs would have bombs strapped to them. A triggering device would set off the bomb when it was below the tank, killing the dog and destroying the tank. However, the weapon did not work well in practice, as the dogs could not reliably distinguish between German and Soviet tanks. Additionally, once German forces realized what was happening, German leaders told all frontline units that any dogs they might encounter should be assumed to be rabid and must be shot.

Hitler, *far left*, inspects an area of Polish resistance, near a heavy Polish long-range gun, on September 21, 1939.

LONG-RANGE DESTRUCTION

Of the many types of weapons used on the battlefields of World War II, long-range cannons, or artillery, proved the deadliest. More than half of the war's battle casualties were the result of artillery fire.[1] Artillery pieces enabled armies to strike targets several miles away. Some shots were carefully aimed and calculated, based on known enemy locations. Others were fired in huge volleys in the enemy's general direction. The complex science of artillery aiming involved a deep understanding of math and physics. However it was fired, artillery fire brought large-scale terror and destruction to those unlucky enough to be caught in its path.

Artillery ranged from tiny mortars, portable tubes used to launch handheld explosives, to enormous cannons that could only be transported by rail and were accompanied by a crew of hundreds.

Between these extremes were a variety of other types, including howitzers and field guns that were towed onto the battlefield, rocket artillery mounted on trucks, and specialized artillery designed to destroy enemy aircraft.

All sides in the war used the same basic artillery, but different nations took significantly different approaches to the development of new artillery weapons. The United States and the United Kingdom each established a single group to select new artillery to design and produce. But in Germany, multiple groups developed competing plans and designs. It led to huge, unwieldy cannons that were useful propaganda tools but ineffective weapons.

DORA

Germany's politicized artillery development process led to the creation of Dora. The 1,350–short ton (1,225 metric ton) cannon rode on twin railway tracks.[3] It fired 31.5-inch (800 mm) shells that weighed 7 short tons (6.3 metric tons) each.[4] Its range was approximately 29 miles (47 km).[5] Moving and firing the weapon required a crew of hundreds of men, making it extremely unwieldy. The military impact of the guns, relative to their enormous cost, was small.

GUNS IN THE FIELD

Midsize US artillery pieces included guns and howitzers. During World War I, the United States had used French and British artillery. After the war, the United States decided to develop a US model. But without an active military conflict, the weapon was not urgently needed. The development of the new weapon was slow. Work was finally finished on the howitzer M1 in 1940.

The M1 fired 200-pound (91 kg) explosive shells more than ten miles (16 km).[2] Lacking a motor, the weapon was towed into position by trucks or tractors.

British howitzers mounted on rails protected the British coastline from attack.

Another towed artillery piece, the US M2A1 howitzer, was a key light howitzer of the war. Firing a 4.1-inch (105 mm) shell, it saw action in both Europe and the Pacific. It featured a versatile firing angle. This allowed it to lob high, arcing shots at enemies on the other side of hills, while also permitting it to fire almost straight ahead to directly target enemy units. If necessary, it could fire at tanks as far as 2,000 yards (1,830 m) away.[6]

The United States introduced larger howitzers as well, with an eight-inch (203 mm) shell and an even bigger 9.4-inch (240 mm) shell. The latter first saw service in early 1944. It was used widely in Allied advances through Italy and northwest Europe. The new model's 360-pound (163 kg) shells easily destroyed reinforced enemy bunkers, but the weapon's firepower came at a cost.[7] After arriving in its designated position, the new M1 took up to eight hours to set up

LITTLE DAVID

The Little David was a mortar developed by the United States. It had the largest caliber of any artillery weapon in World War II. The weapon was originally built to test bombs designed to be dropped from airplanes. Rather than wasting airplane fuel by dropping the bombs from the air, the bombs would be launched into the air by the enormous mortar. As the United States prepared for a potential invasion of the Japanese islands, planners realized the Little David could be useful in smashing bunkers. It was modified to fire shells 36 inches (914 mm) in diameter.[8] However, testing showed the accuracy and range of the weapon were relatively poor. Additionally, setting up the weapon for firing took 12 hours. When the Japanese surrendered in August 1945, the need for such a powerful artillery piece vanished. The Little David was never used in combat.

and prepare for firing. This made it most useful when both sides were stationary for long periods of time.

The best-known British artillery piece of the war in all theaters was the Ordnance QF 25-Pounder, named for the weight of the shells it fired. Its key strength was its ability to be adapted to many different situations. When artillery was needed in the jungles of New Guinea, a smaller, lighter version could more easily move through difficult terrain. A version used in the mountains allowed for a steeper firing angle, making it easier to use on the uneven terrain. The weapon was also employed in North Africa, where it was used at a relatively short range against German tanks. A single soldier could quickly aim the 25-Pounder. This feature was critical when the gun took on an emergency antitank role.

Japanese artillery appeared old to many observers. However, their various types were quite functional, designed for different conflicts than in the West and therefore using different techniques. Japanese artillery also featured a distinct advantage in range compared to similar foreign types of the same weight.

SOVIET ARTILLERY

The Soviet Union's artillery was influenced by the German invasion in 1941. In a matter of months, the Soviet Union lost huge numbers of its artillery pieces. To rebuild their artillery force, the Soviets redesigned their weapons, making them easier to manufacture quickly and adding more interchangeable parts.

One important design was the Field Gun Model 1942, which fired three-inch (76 mm) shells. Developed after 1941, it went on to become the most widely produced artillery weapon of the war. The weapon was relatively lightweight and featured a good range. It used the same ammunition as the Soviet T-34 tank, streamlining the army's supply process.

In addition to its vast artillery, the Soviet Union also made heavy use of rocket weapons. The most common was the M-13, also known as the Katyusha. The weapon consisted of metal rails attached to trucks. Rockets approximately 5.2 inches (13.2 cm) in diameter were attached to the rails.[9] When the rockets were fired, the rails guided them at the correct launch angle. Each truck could launch a full load of 16 rockets in the span of ten seconds.[10] The rockets' accuracy was poor, but the way the Katyushas were used made accuracy relatively unimportant. Huge numbers of the trucks were brought together to launch massive barrages at the same time, raining destruction down upon a huge area.

The Katyusha was used against unsuspecting German invaders after the summer of 1941. The sight and sound of a huge Katyusha was an impressive spectacle, and it was effective in attacking a wide swath of a battlefield at once. Soviet leaders recognized the weapon's potential and ordered mass production. To maintain secrecy and security, the trucks were covered by tarps when not in use.

LOCATING ENEMY ARTILLERY

The key to countering enemy artillery is to determine its location so the opposition can take precise aim to destroy it. Armies developed multiple methods of doing this, and British and US techniques were the most effective. The predictable motion caused by gravity on falling objects allows analysts to trace a shell's flight path back to its source. The British used radar to track shells in flight by 1945. Buried microphones could also detect the vibrations made when enemy artillery fired. Even simply watching for the firing flashes of enemy artillery, either from the ground or from an observation aircraft, helped troops find a weapon's source.

A Katyusha could fire many rockets at a time.

German A7V tanks used in World War I were the ancestors to the more modern tanks used in World War II.

ROLLING ARMOR

The wide-open battlefields of Europe and North Africa made tanks into some of World War II's most important weapons. In 1939 and 1940, their use in Germany's evolving blitzkrieg techniques led to the rapid Nazi conquest of much of Europe. And following the Allied invasion of Normandy, France, in 1944, a seemingly limitless stream of US tanks helped liberate the nations of Western Europe.

The ancestors to these powerful weapons dated back approximately two decades. The tank joined the battlefield halfway through World War I. In September 1916, the United Kingdom deployed its early tanks in an effort to break the bloody stalemate on the European continent. Over the next two years, the slow, heavy weapons helped the allied British and French forces make important breakthroughs against the entrenched Germans. The Allies commissioned lighter and faster tanks with longer ranges to take advantage of these successes and drive deeply into enemy lines. But all types were slow and had frequent mechanical issues.

The German surrender in November 1918 brought the end of World War I. Even in the victorious countries, which included France, the United Kingdom, and the United States, the public was generally against developing and maintaining expensive armies. Some in the militaries also opposed the continued development of tanks. To critics, armored vehicles were seen as a unique consequence of trench warfare, designed only to break through heavily fortified lines. For other situations, some thought tanks might not be the best weapons. A few leaders in cavalry units were against tanks for fear their horse-based units might be replaced.

In contrast, Germany's army leaders were especially interested in the tank's potential during the interwar years. The nation began secretly rearming in the early 1920s, defying the treaty limiting its military power following World War I. In 1933, the German army established a program to build a new, modern tank. The new vehicle was the first in the

THE TREATY OF VERSAILLES

The Treaty of Versailles was signed in June 1919 by Germany and the Allied nations. It officially ended the state of war between them. The treaty included numerous restrictions on the German military, including an outright ban on the construction or import of tanks. Germany's stealthy rearmament began in the 1920s. Germany then developed new tanks under innocuous names to hide their true purpose and avoid publicly breaking the treaty. The Pzkw I was developed as the *landwirtschäftlicher Schlepper*, which means "industrial tractor." The Pzkw IV was known as the *mitteren Traktor*, or "medium tractor."

German Pzkw III with a 1.46-inch (37 mm) gun during a military exercise in November 1938

Panzerkampfwagen (Pzkw) line of tanks. These weapons would go on to define the war's armored battles.

EVOLVING GERMAN ARMOR

The Pzkw I with two machine guns first saw action in Germany's 1939 invasion of Poland. The larger Pzkw II with a small 0.79-inch (20 mm) gun made up the bulk of the German tank force during the May 1940 invasion of France. The Germans later created huge tanks that dwarfed the smaller ones made at the start of the war. The next version, the Pzkw III, was more than twice the weight of the Pzkw II. This size increase was driven by the desire for larger 1.46-inch

A German Pzkw IV tank captured by Allies in North Africa in 1942 shows its damage from shell fire.

(37 mm) guns. Able to fire rounds at high velocity, powerful guns were necessary to defeat enemy armored vehicles. Combat experience in 1940 demanded bigger antitank guns. Yet these larger guns came at a cost. They required a heavier turret to withstand the stress of firing them. The tanks also needed additional storage space for larger ammunition. Big guns eventually drove German tanks to enormous sizes.

Featuring a 2.95-inch (75 mm) cannon, the Pzkw IV was the main German tank of the war. Approximately 9,000 were built.[1] Originally designed to counter enemy infantry, the Pzkw IV later took on an antitank role. Still, the German military sought an even larger and better tank to fight the enormous number of Soviet tanks on the eastern front. The result was the Pzkw V medium tank, better known as the Panther.

The Panther was rushed into production to counter new Soviet threats. Its first major battle was the massive armored clash at the Battle of Kursk in July 1943. The large tank had a 2.95-inch (75 mm) cannon and sloped armor designed to deflect enemy shells. But by the time of the Panther's introduction, Allied bombing was damaging factories and slowing German production capacity. Additionally, Germany had only begun using its full production capacity in 1942, when heavy Soviet resistance made it clear the war would last longer than expected. The Germans intended to produce 600 of the tanks per month, but could only manage to build 330 per month.[2]

In May 1941, one month before the German invasion of the Soviet Union, the German army ordered the design and production of another enormous tank. The Pzkw VI heavy tank, famous as the Tiger I, carried a 3.46-inch (88 mm) cannon. The Tiger's firepower and thick armor were offset by its complexity, which made it difficult to build and maintain. At the same time, Allied bombing continued damaging German efforts to boost tank production. In 1944, a single raid on a factory in the German city of Kassel destroyed 200 newly produced Tigers.[3]

QUANTITY OVER QUALITY

Between the world wars, the future Allied nations noticed Germany's rearmament and launched their own military buildups. They sought to use new weapon technology, including tanks and new fighting techniques, to prevent another trench war similar to World War I. Still, the US tank-building program did not match Germany's. After seeing the speed with which German tanks crushed Poland and France in 1939 and 1940, the US military decided it needed a new, tougher tank. The result was the M3 light tank.

The M3 began rolling off US assembly lines in 1941. The model was equipped with a 1.46-inch (37 mm) cannon, but it soon became clear this would be inadequate against modern German armor. When US M3 crews first entered combat against General Erwin Rommel's larger German tanks in North Africa in November 1942, they quickly realized their tanks' shortcomings. US soldier Freeland A. Daubin recalled his first encounter with a German Pzkw IV:

> *The 37 mm gun of the little American M3 light tank popped and snapped like an angry cap pistol . . . In a frenzy of desperation and fading faith in their highly-touted weapon, the M3 crew pumped more than eighteen rounds at the [German tank] while it came in. Through the scope sight the tracer could be seen to hit, then glance straight up. Popcorn balls thrown by Little Bo Peep would have been just as effective.[4]*

Designers soon looked to bigger tanks, including the M3 Lee medium tank. It had both a 1.46-inch (37 mm) gun and a 2.95-inch (75 mm) gun. The smaller weapon was mounted on the rotating turret. But the larger gun was mounted low in the hull, where it could not independently swivel in all directions. The tank had to be pointed in the direction of fire.

After rushing the M3 medium tank into production, US tank designers drew up plans for a more flexible model that could turn its 2.95-inch (75 mm) cannon in all directions. This new model was the M4 medium tank, commonly known as

ERWIN ROMMEL

1891—1944

German general Erwin Rommel, born on November 15, 1891, was one of the most famous and respected tank commanders of World War II. He first led the Afrika Korps, the famed German tank forces that fought in North Africa. This command cemented his reputation as a bold, principled commander respected not only by his own men but also by his enemies.

Rommel gained the nickname "The Desert Fox" for his shrewd use of surprise attacks in North Africa. He won significant victories in the early months of the campaign, but by the end of 1942, the tide began turning against him. He returned to Germany in March 1942.

In July 1944, Rommel's car was strafed by British fighter planes and knocked off the road in France. Rommel sustained severe head injuries. While he rested, German officers carried out a failed attempt to assassinate Hitler. By 1944, Rommel believed German defeat was inevitable, and he was linked with people seeking to overthrow Hitler. There was no evidence Rommel participated in the plot, but his associations came to light after the failed assassination.

Hitler offered Rommel a choice. He could be executed as a traitor or he could commit suicide. Rommel decided to commit suicide. He died on October 14, 1944.

the Sherman. The Sherman became the most important US and Allied tank of the war. More than 40,000 were built during the war. The United States shipped thousands to its allies, especially the United Kingdom and the Soviet Union, but also to Poles, Czechs, and free French. The Sherman proved highly flexible. Many had specialized features ranging from rocket launchers to flamethrowers and anti-mine devices.

The Sherman was the most powerful US tank yet, but its crews still found it inadequate against German armor. By 1943, Allied military leaders recognized this problem. They modified some Shermans with more powerful guns until heavier tanks were ready. Tankers knew they had to hit German tanks at specific weak spots in order to defeat them. The German Tiger tanks, equipped with 3.46-inch (88 mm) cannons, could knock out Shermans relatively easily. The Tiger's shells were capable of penetrating the outer armor of a Sherman, then bouncing around inside and killing the crew. Additionally, as Allied armies moved across Europe toward Germany, German tank forces had the advantage of being on the defensive. Large tanks and

INCREASING TANK SIZES

Pzkw I: 6.6 short tons (6 metric tons)

Pzkw II: 11 short tons (10 metric tons)

Pzkw III: 24.6 short tons (22.3 metric tons)

Pzkw IV: 27.6 short tons (25 metric tons)

T-34: 28.7 short tons (26 metric tons)

M3 Lee: 30 short tons (27.2 metric tons)

Sherman: 35.6 short tons (32.3 metric tons)

Panther: 50.2 short tons (45.5 metric tons)

Tiger: 60.6 short tons (55 metric tons)[5]

Sherman tanks mounted with British guns advance in a French village on July 17, 1944.

antitank weapons could be hidden or camouflaged and attack advancing Allied forces suddenly and without warning.

It typically took four Shermans to defeat one enemy tank. Two attempted to draw the Germans' fire while two flanked the enemy and tried to hit the weaker armor at the German tanks' sides and rear. In the process, many Shermans were destroyed and their crews killed. Sherman tank units especially learned the value of coordination with friendly infantry, artillery, and aircraft to defeat enemy tanks.

The vulnerability of Shermans drew harsh criticism back in the United States. Newspapers ran editorials criticizing the tanks and demanding congressional investigations on their weaknesses. General Dwight D. Eisenhower responded to these criticisms by explaining that it would be logistically difficult to ship larger, heavier tanks to Europe from factories in the United States. He claimed adapted Shermans could use specialized tactics to knock out German armor. Adaptations included heavier guns that could penetrate the front of a German tank, depending upon the gun, ammo type, range, and target. For example, the Allies adapted Shermans to use the long British 17-pounders and US three-inch (76 mm) guns.

HOBART'S FUNNIES

Many specially modified tanks, including Shermans, were in the British 79th Armored Division under the command of Major General Percy Hobart. Their innovative designs helped save Allied lives. The odd-looking tanks became known as Hobart's Funnies. One type featured a large rotating drum held in front of the tank. Heavy chains attached to the drum. As the drum spun and the chains beat the ground, the device set off pressure-sensitive mines without causing damage to the tank. Another type of tank deployed Bangalore torpedoes. These long explosive pipes were pushed through minefields or barbed wire obstacles. Then the tank crew detonated the pipes to clear a path. However, British tanker D. V. Ager recalled these did not always work as planned: "We would duly hook onto the end of the pipe and push. Can you imagine trying to push a narrow flexible pipe cross-country in a straight line? Almost invariably the pipe would describe an elegant arc and come back to menace the operators."[6]

The Soviet T-34/76 tank

SOVIET ARMOR

The Soviet T-34 medium tank entered production in 1940, a year before the Germans invaded the Soviet Union and the country joined the Allies in the war.

The design and production of the T-34 were kept secret, so its appearance on the battlefield came as a surprise to German invaders. The tank's sloped armor, a new feature on tanks at the time, helped make it resistant to enemy fire. Its three-inch (76 mm) cannon was effective against all German tanks it faced.

THE BATTLE OF KURSK
TANK-ON-TANK FIGHTING

The Battle of Kursk was likely history's largest tank-on-tank battle. By the spring of 1943, the momentum on the eastern front had turned against the German forces. The Soviet military pushed the German invaders westward, back across the Soviet Union toward Germany. In July, a Soviet advance formed a bulge in the front lines centered around the city of Kursk, Russia.

The Germans, seeking to stifle Soviet attempts to mount a new offensive, decided to strike this bulge. A massive force would attack from the north and south, cutting off the bulge from Soviet reinforcements and surrounding it with hostile German units. Approximately 900,000 German troops and 2,700 German tanks organized for the attack.[7]

However, the Soviets had predicted the German plan. They withdrew a large portion of their troops and vehicles from the bulge, leaving behind minefields and fortified positions. Then Soviet artillery behind Soviet lines opened fire as the Germans prepared to strike against the bulge. The Germans pressed onward into the bulge, but their attack failed on July 5 in the face of the Soviet preparations. The Soviet forces then launched a massive counterattack with more than 1 million troops and more than 3,000 tanks.[8]

The battle was chaotic. Huge groups of tanks collided at the front lines, opening fire at close range. Survival depended on a crew's ability to quickly rotate their tank's turret into position and fire first. The Soviet Union won a decisive victory.

NORWAY

SWEDEN

DENMARK

POLAND

GERMANY

CZECHOSLOVAKIA

AUSTRIA HUNGARY

CROATIA

ROMANIA

SERBIA

SOVIET UNION

• Kursk

Eastern Front
German Advance

Russian infantry and tanks battled against the Germans on the eastern front in 1942.

However, there were some problems with its construction. Sloppy welding left the tank leaky in wet weather, damaging equipment and ammunition inside. It had relatively soft armor. The radios were also poor, if tanks had them at all, making it difficult to coordinate with other tanks and ground troops.

Soviet factories could quickly build thousands of the tanks to confront the Germans. Some tanks were even left unpainted to get them into action sooner. With continued improvement, the T-34 ultimately became one of the weapons that turned the tide of the war against Germany.

Still, as with the Shermans, Soviet tankers needed to land precise shots to defeat the largest German tanks. One crewman recalled a fight with a German Panther in which a carefully timed shot resulted in a victory:

> *Not once did the German show them his sides or rear to shoot at. Then there was just one instant when the withdrawing Panther hit a small bump and its long gun soared into the air, and it showed its belly. This was the moment that Sergeant Bragin had been patiently waiting for and he whistled an armor-piercing shell at that exposed place. Flames spurted from the German tank, and the Panther of the noted ace began to burn.*[9]

Sherman and T-34 tanks often struggled to defeat their biggest German counterparts. German tank designers continued to develop larger and more powerful tanks through the last years of the war. Yet the high-quality German tanks were ultimately overwhelmed by the numerous Allied tanks on the battlefield. At the same time, mechanical issues plagued German tanks and Germany experienced late-war fuel shortages. For the United States and the Soviet Union, industrial capacity, reliability, and capable supply systems were integral in the victory of their tanks during World War II.

A German crew lines a Type VII U-boat submarine as it enters a German naval base in 1939.

THE WAR AT SEA

Control of the sea was critically important during World War II. Tanks, infantry, and artillery helped troops seize and hold ground, but a nation in command of the oceans could ship soldiers and weapons to critical invasion beaches and battlefields. It could maintain supply chains of fuel, food, and ammunition that stretched halfway across the world. Much of the war's naval activity revolved around protecting friendly cargo ships and sinking enemy vessels.

In the Atlantic Ocean, German submarines attacked a seemingly endless stream of cargo from the United States and Canada to the United Kingdom and the Soviet Union. In the Pacific Ocean, US submarines raided Japan's ships among the remote islands of eastern Asia. The forces in both seas also operated huge fleets of surface ships, ranging from cruisers and destroyers to mighty battleships.

THE GROWING US NAVY

Each year, the number of US ships in service increased:

June 30, 1940	1,099
June 30, 1941	1,899
June 30, 1942	5,612
June 30, 1943	18,493
June 30, 1944	46,032
June 30, 1945	67,952[1]

During the decades leading up to the war, Japan's navy went from being second-tier to being a formidable force. In response, the US Navy began modernizing and upgrading its fleet in the 1930s, most of which came into service during World War II. The industrial capacity of the United States meant the size and quality of US fleets outpaced Japan's once the war began.

SUBMARINES

World War II submarines were still surface vessels. They submerged for short periods only. The two leading Axis powers used submarines in different ways. Japanese submarines targeted Allied warships, while German vessels focused on sinking Allied cargo ships. The two strategies brought dramatically different results. German submarines, known as U-boats, sank approximately 2,000 supply ships over the course of the war. Japanese subs sank fewer than 20 US warships.[2]

At the beginning of the war, Germany's submarine fleet was relatively small. Following World War I, when German subs menaced merchant shipping on the Atlantic, the Allies forced Germany to surrender all of its U-boats. They also banned Germany from building new submarines. After Hitler came to power, he

A two-man Japanese submarine, damaged during the Pearl Harbor attack, beached at Waimanalo, Hawaii, in 1941.

ignored the restrictions and launched a new shipbuilding program. In 1939, this new fleet consisted of fewer than 60 U-boats.[3]

During the war, the Allies developed more effective antisubmarine weapons. The key to defeating an enemy submarine was to attack quickly when it was near the surface. Torpedoes, guns, bombs dropped from aircraft, and simple ramming destroyed enemy submarines. If a submarine crew had time to react, a submarine could dive to safety in the deeper ocean.

Destroying submarines underwater was more difficult, but it was possible. Depth charges, explosives enclosed within containers capable of withstanding the crushing pressure of the ocean, could be dropped from surface ships in an attempt to hit enemy subs. Accuracy was difficult to achieve, so many depth charges were dropped in set patterns to increase the chance of getting hits. The weapon could even be effective when it missed. The sound and force generated by the nearby explosions reverberated through targeted submarines, damaging hulls and affecting the crew's morale. Subs under attack were forced to remain deep underwater, where they could not attack enemy surface ships. Depth charges were responsible for nearly half of U-boat losses.[4]

In response to the Allies' advances in antisubmarine warfare, Germany adopted a new submarine tactic known as the wolf pack. Before, submarines would operate

TORPEDOES

Stealthy submarines could hide underwater, but their torpedoes made them deadly. Each torpedo is essentially a small, unmanned submarine with an explosive attached to it. Torpedoes usually contain mechanisms that keep them at the proper depth and steer them in the desired direction. Typical torpedoes from World War II measured up to 20 feet (6.1 m) long and could strike targets a few miles away.[5] However, successfully attacking targets at this range was very difficult. Torpedoes using oil or alcohol as fuels left a wake on the surface as they moved, giving a targeted ship time to react and steer out of the way. Later electric models, powered by batteries, left no wake and were harder to evade. The Japanese developed a large, powerful, oxygen-fueled torpedo model known to historians as the Long Lance. It sank more than a dozen Allied warships in the Pacific.

independently to attack enemy convoys. Under the new tactic, submarines worked in coordinated teams. One U-boat tracked the movement of a convoy, and its fellow ships carried out night attacks on merchant vessels. This new tactic worked well at first, but the Allies soon adapted to it. Radar technology made it possible to detect U-boats at a distance, and more armed escort ships accompanied convoys. U-boat losses began mounting. In May 1943, 41 were sunk.[6] For the rest of the war, U-boats were used mostly in remote parts of the ocean where they could attack less protected targets. In all, the Allies sunk 781 U-boats—a full 66 percent of those in service.[7]

By contrast, US submarines in the Pacific Ocean became more effective as the war went on. They focused on Japanese shipping vessels to cause severe supply shortages and hopefully hasten Japanese surrender. By 1944, US subs made use of tactics similar to the German wolf pack, and they were sinking one ship for every ten torpedoes fired.[8] Though submarine crews represented less than 2 percent of the US Navy's personnel, they were responsible for 55 percent of Japan's shipping losses.[9]

THE GREAT BATTLESHIPS

Battleships were the centerpieces of the world's leading navies at the outset of World War II. These massive ships had large guns to engage in naval battles against enemy battleships. The guns could also support beach landings by infantry, as they did during many island invasions in the Pacific.

The top US battleships of the war belonged to the Iowa class. These ships were designed with speed in mind, since they needed to be able to keep up with the new, fast aircraft carriers. Still, the Iowa class was heavily armed

The USS *Iowa* in the Pacific Ocean on November 8, 1944

and armored. Each ship was equipped with nine guns firing 16-inch (40.6 cm) diameter shells. Their armor plating was more than 12 inches (30.5 cm) thick in places.[10]

When designing its battleships, Japan recognized the United States would likely be able to produce larger quantities of vessels. Instead, Japan would try to win through quality. The result was its Yamato-class battleships, which would become the largest battleships in naval history. Most of the nation's other battleships were older, prewar designs, but the Yamato vessels were among the most advanced battleships on the seas.

International treaties signed in the decades following World War I had attempted to limit the size and strength of the world's navies. One treaty required battleships to displace fewer than 35,000 short tons (31,750 metric tons) and carry guns with a maximum caliber of 16 inches.[11] Desiring much larger vessels, Japan's naval authorities launched a secret development program, planning to unveil its new ships only after the treaty expired in 1940.

The first of two ships in the Yamato class, called the *Yamato*, was finished only a week after the Japanese attack on the US naval base at Pearl Harbor in December 1941. The *Yamato* displaced 70,000 short tons (64,000 metric tons), and its guns measured 18.1 inches (46 cm) in diameter.[12] Operating the ship required a crew of 2,500 men.[13]

In the end, the *Yamato* was unable to halt the advance of the giant US fleets. As the United States landed on Okinawa, a group of islands just south of the Japanese homeland, the desperate Japanese navy sent the *Yamato* on a suicide mission against the invading force. The ship carried only enough fuel for a one-way voyage, and it lacked aerial protection from friendly fighters. Aircraft from US carriers located and sank the ship hundreds of miles from Okinawa on April 7, 1945.

SINKING THE *BISMARCK*

The German navy placed less emphasis on surface ships than the United States and Japan, but it still possessed two powerful battleships, the *Bismarck* and the *Tirpitz*. The *Bismark*'s destruction by British forces highlighted the vulnerability of battleships. In May 1941, a British carrier aircraft located and attacked the *Bismarck*. A torpedo dropped from an aircraft struck the ship, disabling its steering and leaving it helpless against the British fleet that arrived the next morning. The ability of relatively tiny aircraft to defeat enormous, expensive ships was a key factor that forced naval planners to reconsider the central position of battleships in their fleets.

A squadron of Douglas Devastator torpedo bombers gets ready for takeoff aboard a US aircraft carrier on June 4, 1942.

THE RISE OF CARRIERS

At the war's beginning, battleships dominated the world's major navies. With their powerful guns and thickly armored hulls, battleships could destroy smaller vessels and bombard enemy shorelines. As the war progressed, a new type of ship began eclipsing the battleship. Aircraft carriers enabled a nation's forces to attack enemy ships hundreds of miles away without putting their own vessels in danger.

Carriers fulfilled a wide variety of roles in the world's naval forces. Their planes could fly hundreds of miles to locate enemy fleets. Carrier-based torpedo planes could sink enemy battleships and carriers. A carrier's bombers could destroy ground targets along shores. Its fighter planes could defend a carrier from enemy aircraft. Carriers could provide air cover for battleships, allowing battleships to approach the enemy and open fire with their huge guns. Carriers, especially the smaller designs, could also help escort cargo convoys and protect them from enemy fire in the air and on the sea.

Just three nations used aircraft carriers during the war: the United States, the United Kingdom, and Japan. France had one, but the nation surrendered in 1940. Italy and Germany had vessels under construction, but none were completed in time to join the conflict. Hermann Göring, the head of Germany's Luftwaffe, or air force, refused to let the German navy develop aircraft units. This rivalry between the branches of the German military prevented the nation from establishing a carrier force.

Carriers changed the nature of the war at sea. In the Atlantic, small escort carriers stocked with antisubmarine aircraft helped neutralize the U-boat threat. Carriers fought in the Pacific when Japanese planes struck Pearl Harbor. Throughout the conflict, Japanese and US carriers and their planes battled for control of not just the sea, but also the air above the sea. The Battle of the Coral Sea, fought in May 1942, became the first naval battle in history in which the opposing fleets never saw each other.

PROJECT HABBAKUK

Desperate to defend merchant ships against the threat of U-boats, the United Kingdom sought a way to provide its vessels with air cover. In 1942, it did not possess enough aircraft carriers to carry out this role. A British scientist developed an unusual idea to protect shipping: aircraft carriers made out of ice. He named the plan Project Habbakuk, after a biblical character. The scheme called for enormous floating runways made up of a mixture of ice and paper pulp. When a bomb or torpedo hit the carrier, the plan said, repairs could be made by simply pouring water into the damaged area and freezing it. The project got as far as a model built on a lake in Canada. However, rising costs, technical problems, and the building of normal carriers led to the cancellation of the project in 1943.

DOOLITTLE'S RAID

As the United States readied for war in the Pacific, thousands of miles lay between its air bases and the Japanese islands. US forces were years away from being able to strike Japan. But an aircraft carrier, the *Hornet*, made it possible for the United States to stage a daring raid on Tokyo, the Japanese capital, in April 1942. After the *Hornet* approached within several hundred miles of the islands, 16 specially trained crews took off in B-25 bombers from its deck. These aircraft usually flew from bases on land, but the carrier was just long enough for them to get airborne. They traveled to Japan on missions to bomb Tokyo and other cities. The damage they caused was relatively insignificant, but the raid provided a morale boost for US forces and civilians on the home front.

CARRIERS IN THE PACIFIC

When the war began, the US Navy possessed seven aircraft carriers. In a stroke of luck, none of them were present at Pearl Harbor during the Japanese attack. Within a year, Japanese fleets had destroyed four of them in battle. The low point of the US carrier force came in January 1943, when only one active carrier remained afloat. US shipyards worked overtime to replace these losses with new Essex-class carriers.

The new carriers featured accurate radar-controlled antiaircraft guns and many improvements so they could accommodate the new, larger, and heavier aircraft in service. Each Essex-class carrier was designed to carry 82 aircraft.[1] However, wartime adaptations enabled them to carry up to 108 planes.[2] The ships could carry enough fuel to travel 17,000 miles (27,400 km).[3] A crew of more than 3,200 was needed to operate each of the floating air bases.[4]

BATTLE OF THE CORAL SEA
AIR-SEA FIGHTING IN THE PACIFIC

The Battle of the Coral Sea was fought between the United States and Japan in May 1942. The battle happened just months into the war in the Pacific. Japan's winning momentum was carrying it from conquest to conquest. The expanding empire turned its attention to the Coral Sea, just northeast of Australia. It sought to invade New Guinea at Port Moresby, giving it air bases within striking distance of Australia.

US naval leaders learned about Japan's plans and were determined to prevent the invasion. They dispatched carriers and other ships to the area. On May 7, each side's planes found the opposing fleet. One US destroyer was sunk, while US planes destroyed a Japanese light carrier. The next day, Japanese planes sank the US carrier *Lexington* and severely damaged the *Yorktown*. In return, US aircraft hit the Japanese carrier *Shokaku*, damaging it badly enough that it had to return to Japan for repairs.

Both sides suffered severe losses in the battle, but US commanders achieved their goal. The withdrawal of the wounded Japanese carrier force meant the remaining invading ships lacked the aerial protection needed to go forward with the Japanese invasion. The carrier-versus-carrier combat seen at the Coral Sea would become more common over the course of the war in the Pacific.

Crew members escaped the USS *Lexington* after it was hit by Japanese bombs and torpedoes during the Battle of the Coral Sea.

Among the most powerful Japanese carriers were those in the Shokaku class. These vessels incorporated the latest design features. Each ship could carry 75 planes, which were launched using two separate aircraft catapults.[5] The notable weakness of the Shokaku class was its vulnerable stocks of aviation fuel. This may have contributed to the torpedo sinking of the class's lead ship, the *Shokaku*, at the Battle of the Philippine Sea, which occurred east of the Philippines in June 1944.

AIRPOWER AT SEA

The capacity and capabilities of US and Japanese carriers were important, but the critical factor in carrier warfare was the quality of the planes they carried and the skill of the pilots. Early in the war, Japan led in both of these areas. Japanese pilots were experienced and well trained. Their Mitsubishi A6M, better known as the Zero, was among the best carrier-based aircraft in the world at the start of the war.

The Zero was designed in 1937 and first flew two years later. It boasted high speed, long range, and excellent maneuverability. The lightness required to achieve these attributes meant the plane was poorly armored and fragile under enemy fire. Still, the ability to climb and turn quickly gave Japan air superiority in early battles over the Pacific.

By contrast, the United States struggled in carrier warfare in the months following Pearl Harbor. Its pilots were skilled, but the available carrier planes, including the Grumman F4F Wildcat, failed to match up to the Zeros. The United States' use of radar during the early phase of the war was also much less effective than it would become in the conflict's later years.

US aircraft carriers, including an Essex-class carrier (*second in line*), return to the Caroline Islands on December 12, 1944, after action in the Philippines.

The combination of the new Essex-class carriers, increasing experience, and a new model of carrier fighter planes helped turn the tide against the Japanese in the Pacific. The new fighter, the Grumman F6F Hellcat, was designed to counter Zeros. The Hellcat's powerful engine enabled it to make tighter turns,

A Hellcat prepares for takeoff in the Pacific in 1943.

steeper dives, and sharper climbs than the Zero. Still, its designers were able to incorporate durable armor. In one incident, a Hellcat landed safely on its carrier with approximately 200 bullet holes.[6]

The Hellcats arrived in the Pacific in August 1943 and soon proved capable of handling the Zero in combat. In the course of the war, Hellcats downed 5,163 enemy aircraft.[7] This represented close to three-quarters of all US Navy kills.[8]

Just 270 Hellcats were lost.[9] US pilot Ted Winters recalled later that Japanese pilots began fearing the Hellcat:

> *Most of our kills were from the rear end. [The Japanese] are scared to death of the Grummans. Only when they outnumber you terrifically will they even stay near you. They will make passes, but stay far away and scram when you turn on them.*[10]

As Japan lost more and more of its skilled pilots, it was unable to train new ones fast enough to replace them. By late 1944, the average Japanese carrier pilot had approximately 40 hours of flying experience.[11] His US counterpart had approximately 525 hours.[12] Losses of aircraft, carriers, and carrier crews compounded Japan's problems. As a result, the Japanese carrier force became ineffective. At the Battle of Leyte Gulf in the Philippines in October 1944, Japanese forces used carriers as bait to draw US carriers away from the main action. By that time, nearly 100 US carriers were in service, ranging from large fleet carriers, such as those of the Essex-class, to smaller light and escort carriers.[13] An average of one new carrier was being completed at shipyards each week.[14]

CARRIER VULNERABILITY

The United States and Japan faced off in the central Pacific Ocean at the Battle of Midway in early June 1942. The US won a decisive victory, sinking four of Japan's valuable carriers. The battle highlighted the vulnerability of carriers. On June 4, dive bombers from the US carrier *Enterprise* spotted Japanese carriers at sea. A force of 37 Douglas SBD Dauntless dive bombers struck, sinking three carriers.[15] Subsequent attacks sank the fourth carrier later that day. The US Navy had struck a massive blow to Japan's carrier fleet.

A group of British Vickers Wellington long-range medium bombers on February 8, 1940

WINNING THE SKY

When World War I began in 1914, the airplane was a relatively new invention. During the war, there were significant advances in technology and battle tactics, but airplanes were still a minor part of battlefield victories. Planes were still canvas-covered biplanes with two wings, open cockpits, and small engines. In the decades following the conflict, technological improvements developed rapidly. Newer aircraft could fly faster, climb higher, and carry more bombs.

Until World War II, these new aircraft had not been tested on a large scale. The war involved airplanes from the beginning, as Hitler's Stukas rained bombs upon Polish forces during the 1939 invasion. From those opening moments onward, airpower played a decisive role in World War II. Two major classes of aircraft fought in the skies over Europe and Asia: fighters and bombers.

FIGHTER PLANES

The role of fighter planes was to shoot down enemy fighters and bombers, defend friendly bombers, and sometimes provide support for ground forces using machine guns and cannons or small bombs. World War II fighters differed dramatically from more primitive planes used in the previous world war. Most of the new fighters were high-performance monoplanes with powerful engines. They had landing gear that could retract within the body of the aircraft during flight. Enclosed cockpits meant pilots could safely fly to high altitudes.

Fighters were responsible for an Allied victory in one of the war's most critical battles. By the summer of 1940, German armies had successfully conquered France and Poland. Their presence in France put them within miles of the British coastline, just across the narrow English Channel. Germany planned to invade the United Kingdom, calling it Operation Sea Lion. However, German planners knew they would need to achieve air superiority over the United Kingdom to stand any chance of success. Otherwise planes from Britain's Royal Air Force (RAF) could quickly destroy an invading force.

AIRCRAFT PRODUCTION

Few weapons from World War II demonstrated the superiority of US production capacity as well as aircraft. Compared to guns and tanks, aircraft are incredibly complex. A typical car from the World War II era had approximately 15,000 parts.[1] By comparison, a B-24 bomber had 1.55 million parts.[2] Yet once US factories ramped up aircraft production, a single factory could complete one B-24 every 63 minutes.[3] The United States built fewer than 2,000 aircraft in 1938, but more than 96,000 in 1944.[4]

The German Messerschmitt Bf 110 was armed with machine guns and cannons.

The German Luftwaffe attempted to neutralize the RAF threat by launching bombing raids on air bases within the United Kingdom in the late summer. It sent its Messerschmitt Bf 109 fighters to protect its bombers. First flown in September 1935, the Bf 109 was an effective fighter, but it had one fatal weakness: short range with a limited fuel capacity. Once it reached London, a Bf 109 had enough fuel for only ten minutes of fighting before it had to return across the English Channel.

Countering the Bf 109 was one of the most effective fighters of the war: the British Supermarine Spitfire. The Spitfire was equipped with the Merlin engine, built by car manufacturer Rolls-Royce. The Merlin made the Spitfire extremely fast, especially at high altitudes, where it would fight Bf 109s. It could reach speeds of more than 360 miles per hour (580 kmh).[5] Spitfires were also short-range aircraft, but they fought over home ground, giving them more battle time than the Bf 109s. The Hawker Hurricane, another British fighter, focused on German bombers. Equipped with eight machine guns, the Hurricane could slice through groups of enemy aircraft. The RAF and its pilots successfully defended the United Kingdom, with help from the Czechs, Poles, and French who had escaped Europe. Lacking control of the air, Germany was forced to call off its invasion.

The Bf 109 was not the only aircraft that struggled with a limited range during World War II. As the Allies launched bombing raids deep within Germany, their existing fighters were unable to escort the bombers the entire way. This led to severe bomber losses. To give bombers a fighting chance, a long-range fighter was needed.

The P-51 Mustang was the answer to the Allies' problems. The aircraft was originally designed in 1940, and early models proved too slow to be effective. When a few were shipped to the United Kingdom for testing, test pilots suggested using the Merlin engine in Mustangs to boost their performance. At first, their suggestions were ignored. Bureaucratic issues, great competition for resources, and skeptics slowed the engine's acceptance.

An RAF Mustang

US factories had the ability to mass-produce the Merlin-equipped Mustang, but rivalries between airplane manufacturers didn't allow that to happen.

Finally, after a series of catastrophic bombing raids, in which large numbers of unescorted Allied bombers were shot down over Europe, the Mustang program moved forward. Mustangs with Merlin engines were ready for battle by December 1943, and they soon proved to be excellent fighter airplanes. External fuel tanks could be dropped when empty. This gave the fighters outstanding range, enabling them to accompany bombers deep into Germany. In all, the United States built more than 15,000 Mustangs.[6]

BOMBING CITIES

The most destructive weapons of World War II were the Allied bomber formations that flew over Germany and Japan. Groups of US and British bombers included the Avro Lancaster, Handley Page Halifax, Boeing B-17 Flying Fortress, Boeing B-24 Liberator, and Boeing B-29 Superfortress. Together they destroyed Axis cities, railroads, and factories. They also destroyed the resources and facilities the Axis powers needed to wage war and killed hundreds of thousands of German and Japanese civilians.

As did the Spitfire and the Mustang, the Lancaster used the Merlin engine. With four Merlins pushing it across the sky, the Lancaster was able to carry the largest bombs of the war—the British earthquake bombs—designed to penetrate deeply before detonation. The Tallboy weighed 12,000 pounds (5,500 kg), and the Grand Slam weighed 22,000 pounds (10,000 kg).[7] These bombs struck important German infrastructure, including bridges and submarine docks.

The United States' Flying Fortress got its name from the array of Browning's 0.5-inch (12.7 mm) M2 defensive machine guns mounted in its nose, and tail and along its sides and bottom. These guns made it possible for a Flying Fortress to defend itself against enemy fighters. US military leaders believed this would permit bombers to safely strike enemy targets during daylight hours without escorts. However, mounting losses of bombers proved this wrong. Crew members had to fly 25 missions before being eligible to be rotated off combat. In 1943, only one in three crew members would survive that long.[8]

Technical Sergeant Earl Burke served as a ball-turret gunner in a Flying Fortress. These crew members sat in a ball mounted below the bomber and

AIR FORMATION

Before the arrival of long-range fighter escorts in Europe, US bombers defended themselves by flying in compact formations. In doing so, they could concentrate their machine gun fire at enemy fighters. The bombers could also minimize the target size for enemy fighters attempting head-on attacks. One typical formation involved 54 bombers. In this formation, three groups of 18 aircraft joined together. The aircraft fit in a space 2,200 yards (2,000 m) wide and 880 yards (800 m) deep.[10] Just 600 yards (550 m) separated the first plane from the last one.[11]

defended the plane against enemy fighters from below. Burke later recalled the conditions he faced:

> You put your knees up against your ears almost like a fetal position. You're up there, jammed in that little thing, and you've got these horrendous machine guns in front of you—fifty-millimeter, two of them. And you've got a radio in there. You've got oxygen. And you can hook up your electrical suit to keep warm. That was it.[9]

The B-29 Superfortress was a quantum leap in technology and weighed approximately twice as much as the Flying Fortress. The huge aircraft sometimes struggled to take off, but once it began climbing, its high speed and altitude made it very difficult for enemy fighters to reach it. Too large for typical European runways, the B-29 was exclusively used against Japan, taking off from island runways built as US forces swept across the Pacific Ocean.

US General Curtis LeMay, seeking to devastate Japan, ordered low-altitude Superfortress raids on Japanese cities using incendiary bombs. The threat from Japanese fighters had been reduced by Japan's losses of planes and pilots, so

Two Superfortresses released bombs at their target, a Japanese supply depot, on March 17, 1945.

Superfortresses often had most of their defensive machine guns removed so they could carry more bombs.[12]

Many Japanese houses were constructed from wood, so massive firestorms triggered by the bombs spread quickly and widely, causing far more damage than conventional bombs. On March 9, 1945, a raid on Tokyo destroyed approximately 16 square miles (41 sq km) of the city, killing up to 130,000 people.[13] By the end of the war, the Superfortresses were virtually invincible over Japan. In the final major bombing raid, on August 14, 1945, 800 Superfortresses dropped their incendiary bombs on Isesaki in central Japan.[14] All of the planes returned to base unharmed. These extreme measures demonstrated the meaning of total war in the age of long-range bombers. The civilians themselves had become targets.

THE IMPORTANCE OF PILOTS

As Germany and Japan discovered in the later years of the war, a lack of skilled pilots can doom an air force, even when its aircraft are of high quality. During the Battle of Britain, UK leader Winston Churchill recognized the importance of pilots to victory:

> All hearts go out to the fighter pilots, whose brilliant actions we see with our own eyes day after day; but we must never forget that all the time, night after night, month after month, our bomber squadrons travel far into Germany, find their targets in the darkness by the highest navigational skill, aim their attacks, often under the heaviest fire, often with serious loss, with deliberate, careful discrimination, and inflict shattering blows upon the whole of the technical and war-making structure of the Nazi power.[15]

Both the United States and the United Kingdom had quickly recognized the need for comprehensive training programs to train many new pilots to fight a long war.

A Japanese kamikaze pilot crashed his plane into the ocean after missing his target, a US light carrier, on May 4, 1945.

CHAPTER

9

A BLOODY END

As the Allies closed in on all fronts, the Axis powers attempted to find ways to prevent their seemingly inevitable defeat. In some cases, they turned in desperation to suicidal weapons. Other developments focused on rushing advanced technology onto the battlefield, including jet aircraft and guided missiles. In the end, these measures failed to prevent an Axis defeat. Instead, a technical accomplishment of the United States—the atomic bomb—brought history's deadliest war to a violent end.

WEAPONS OF DESPERATION

In late 1944, the situation was dire for Japan's military. Too many of its skilled pilots were dead, and new Allied planes outclassed Japan's aircraft. Japanese Vice-Admiral Takijiro Onishi introduced a dramatic change in strategy. Rather than trying to drop bombs or torpedoes on the enemy, Japanese pilots intentionally crashed their aircraft into US ships. The attacks became known as kamikaze, or "divine wind."

Kamikaze required much less training than fighter pilots, since they did not need to dogfight, drop bombs accurately, or land. Instead, they were instructed to constantly shift back and forth in the air as they flew toward US fleets, making it difficult for their enemies to tell which ship the kamikaze pilots were targeting. US antiaircraft gunners and fighter pilots shot down most kamikaze pilots, but approximately 20 percent managed to hit Allied ships.[1]

In all, kamikaze pilots sank 27 ships and damaged a further 164.[2]

Onishi believed such suicidal attacks, carried out on a broad scale, could turn the tide of the war: "If we are prepared to sacrifice twenty million Japanese lives in 'special attacks,' victory will be ours."[3] The US Navy losses during the fight for Okinawa was its highest-ever casualty rate. The suicide strikes damaged Allied morale, but they ultimately did little to slow the advance toward Japan.

VENGEANCE WEAPONS

Like Japan, Germany sought weapons so powerful they might single-handedly shift the course of the war. The German military

BALLOON BOMBS

Japan attempted to spread fear within the United States with one desperate tactic. Between November 1944 and March 1945, it released thousands of balloons attached to bombs. Japan hoped that prevailing winds over the Pacific Ocean would carry the bombs to the mainland United States, where they would explode, kill civilians, and cause a panic. Nearly 300 of the bombs were found in Mexico, Canada, and the United States.[4] Only one was deadly: a bomb in Oregon exploded when a woman and five children approached it. All six died. They were the only Americans killed on the mainland by enemy weapons during the war.

US troops captured a German train carrying nine V-2 missiles on April 6, 1945.

funded advanced aircraft and rocket technology. The best-known results of this research are the Vergeltungswaffen, or "retaliation weapons." They included the V-1 flying bomb and the V-2 ballistic missile.

The V-1 looked somewhat like an ordinary aircraft, but it required no pilot. A new type of engine known as a pulse-jet powered it. Explosives were located in the front and a simple guidance system steered the bomb toward its target, which could be many miles from its launching point.

The first V-1 was launched against London on June 13, 1944. By the end of the month, it had been followed by more than 2,400 V-1 flying bombs.[5] The bombs flew slowly enough that it was possible for fighters to shoot them down, and approximately one-third were destroyed or crashed before reaching the British coast. Another third were downed over the British countryside. The rest successfully struck London and the surrounding area. In all, the V-1s killed 6,184 people.[6] The death toll was significant, but far less than had been killed by ordinary bombing.

The V-1 had been an impressive display of technology, but the V-2 was far beyond anything else in the world. The V-2 was a large rocket that carried its explosive payload many miles high, then descended in an arc toward its target. It approached from a high angle at an incredible speed, making it essentially impossible to defend against.

Development of the V-2 dated back to the 1920s, when the German Society for Space Travel worked to develop practical rockets. One of the group's engineers, Wernher von Braun, eventually headed rocket research for the Nazis. The treaties signed after World War I banned Germany from owning heavy artillery. Rocket weapons provided the regime with a loophole, allowing them to build long-range weapons that were not technically artillery. Von Braun's effort gained funding from the German army in 1934, and the military spent vast amounts of money developing and producing his war rockets.

WERNHER VON BRAUN

1912–1977

Wernher von Braun was born in Germany in 1912. From a young age, he was fascinated with astronomy and space. As he studied math and engineering, he became determined to someday build rockets that would travel into space. Von Braun joined the German Society for Space Travel in 1930.

Lacking funding and permission to run rocket tests, von Braun and his fellow rocket designers turned to the military for support in 1934. The German military built a facility in Peenemünde, Germany, for the development and testing of military rocket technology. Von Braun headed these efforts. His advanced A-4 rocket design was renamed the V-2 by the Nazi propaganda unit, and Germany launched it against London and other targets.

As the war in Europe was about to end, von Braun and his rocket team surrendered to the United States. The US government recruited them to develop new rockets. He became a US citizen in 1955 and later began working for the National Aeronautics and Space Administration (NASA). At last his rockets were used to send people into space. Von Braun became the first director of the Marshall Space Flight Center in Huntsville, Alabama. He oversaw the development of the Saturn V, the rocket that successfully sent astronauts to the moon in the late 1960s and early 1970s. Von Braun died on June 16, 1977.

JET AIRCRAFT

German rocket technology influenced rocket development in the postwar world, but another German innovation would have an even broader effect. In the spring of 1944, the Luftwaffe introduced the world's first operational jet fighter, the Messerschmitt Me 262. The Me 262's jet engine gave it an enormous speed advantage over planes using propellers. However, its widespread use was delayed, as Hitler insisted the aircraft be modified to carry bombs in addition to the cannons they used to fight other aircraft. Significant numbers of Me 262s did not reach the battlefield until March 1945, too late to make a difference in the war's outcome. But its technology lived on. Since the time of the Me 262, the world's air forces have relied on jet aircraft.

The British government was alarmed when V-2 rockets began striking London in September 1944. At first, the government told the public explosions in the city's gas pipes caused the destruction. From then until early 1945, when Allied armies had overrun the launching sites in Europe, Germany launched approximately five V-2 rockets per day at the United Kingdom. However, the weapons caused relatively little damage in relation to the massive cost of building them.

These weapons were unable to delay the collapse of Hitler's Germany. After successfully invading German-occupied France in the summer of 1944, the Allies made steady progress across Europe. They reached Germany in March 1945. Hitler, aware the war had been lost, committed suicide on April 30. Germany finally surrendered to the Allies on May 7. However, the war was not yet over. In the Pacific, Japan was still fiercely defending its shrinking empire.

ATOMIC WEAPONS

World War II's single most destructive weapon, the atomic bomb, was not used until the war's final days. In the preceding decades, scientists had made great leaps in their knowledge of atoms and radioactivity. Many realized fission, the splitting of atoms, could result in a chain reaction that would unleash a tremendous amount of energy. It became clear to physicists this process could be used to build a powerful bomb.

Several nations, including Germany, the United Kingdom, Japan, and the United States, conducted research into this possibility. The US effort was known as the Manhattan Project. Under the leadership of physicist Robert Oppenheimer, scientists across the United States worked feverishly to build an atomic bomb before Axis scientists could.

History's first atomic bomb was tested on July 16, 1945, in the New Mexico desert. The weapon's core was made of the radioactive element plutonium. Surrounding the plutonium was a carefully shaped arrangement of explosives designed to detonate in just the right way to trigger fission. In the instant the weapon exploded, a fireball expanded outward, and the bomb emitted a harsh blast of radiation. Finally, the bomb generated a blast of air pressure that knocked down any buildings left standing near the testing site.

US President Harry S. Truman made the final decision to use the new weapon against Japan. He hoped the bomb's destructiveness would persuade Japan to surrender. A single B-29 Superfortress dropped an atomic bomb on Hiroshima and Nagasaki, Japan, on two different days in August 1945. Many square miles of both cities were destroyed, and more than 100,000 Japanese civilians died.[7] The

United States hoped this display of force would cause the Japanese to surrender, preventing the need for a bloody land invasion of Japan's home islands. Weeks later, on September 2, 1945, Japan surrendered. Six years and one day after it began, World War II was over.

AN INDUSTRIAL WAR

The successes and failures of weapons in World War II proved the most sophisticated, powerful weapons did not necessarily lead to victory. Weapon quality was important, but the effectiveness of those weapons would be maximized only when combined with strong industrial capacity and economic organization.

US shipyards quickly replaced devastating US carrier losses, while Japan's similar losses carried lasting effects. Japanese industry was able to design modern artillery, but its factories were unable to keep up. It left troops in the field with obsolete models until the end of the war.

From the M1911 pistol to the Katyusha rocket launcher and the B-29 Superfortress, the weapons of World War II took many forms and carried out a vast range of roles. For the Allies, each type of weapon was crucial to victory. The Garand rifle, the bazooka, and the Sherman tank allowed US forces to seize and hold Axis territory. The Spitfire, Lancaster, and B-17 allowed Allied pilots to attack Axis cities and defend their own. The carriers of the Pacific enabled the United States to project its airpower far from its fleets, while US submarines strangled Japanese shipping. World War II weapons made Allied victory possible, but the soldiers, pilots, and sailors who used those weapons to the best advantage truly won the war.

Hiroshima lay in ruins after being hit by the atomic bomb on August 6, 1945.

TIMELINE

1920s–1930s
Germany begins secretly rebuilding its military, defying restrictions put in place following its loss in World War I.

1930s
The United States begins modernization of its naval fleets.

September 1939
Germany invades Poland, starting World War II.

June 1940
German blitzkrieg defeats France.

July 1943
German and Soviet tanks face off at the Battle of Kursk.

August 1943
The Grumman F6F Hellcat carrier-based fighter arrives in the Pacific.

December 1943
P-51 Mustangs with Merlin engines are ready for battle.

June 13, 1944
The first V-1 is launched against London.

Summer 1940

British Spitfire and Hurricane fighters successfully defend the United Kingdom from German bombing.

1942

Germany's MG 42 enters combat.

May 1942

Japan and the United States clash at the Battle of the Coral Sea.

June 1942

The Battle of Midway is fought and Japan loses four carriers.

March 1945

The Me 262, history's first operational jet fighter aircraft, enters service with Germany.

March 9, 1945

Massive US firebombing raids on Tokyo kill up to 130,000 people.

April 7, 1945

The Japanese battleship Yamato is sunk on its way to Okinawa.

August 1945

The United States drops atomic bombs on the Japanese cities of Hiroshima and Nagasaki.

ESSENTIAL FACTS

KEY PLAYERS

- Adolf Hitler's military buildup makes German rearmament public.

- John Browning designs many of the guns used by the Allies during World War II, including the M1911 pistol and M2 machine gun.

- Erwin Rommel makes effective use of tanks in Europe and North Africa.

- Takijiro Onishi oversees the use of kamikaze suicide attacks in the Pacific.

- Wernher von Braun develops the rocket technology behind the V-2.

KEY STATISTICS

- The United States produces a total of 296,000 aircraft and 86,333 tanks during the war.

- The German MG 42 machine gun fires up to 1,550 rounds per minute.

- The German Tiger tank weighs 60.6 short tons (55 metric tons). The US Sherman tank weighs 35.6 short tons (32.3 metric tons).

- The Japanese battleship *Yamato* is crewed by 2,500 men.

KEY WEAPONS

Early in the war, Stuka dive bombers help Germany conquer Poland and France. When Germany turns its sights to the United Kingdom, Spitfire and Hurricane fighters successfully defend the skies over London. Japan's attack on Pearl Harbor is made possible by its aircraft carriers. US submarines later strangle Japan by cutting its lines of shipping. The war's most powerful weapons—atomic bombs—strike the final major blows of the war.

IMPACT ON THE WAR

The weapons of World War II make it unlike any war that has come before. Civilians, often insulated from wartime violence in the past, find themselves under fire from massive long-range bomber raids. The increasing sophistication of weapons in the 1940s means building a powerful military requires an enormous investment of money and effort, with complex organizations to carry out their use.

QUOTE

"Suddenly there was the roar of an aeroplane. The pilot circled, descending to a height of fifty meters. As he dropped his bombs and fired his machine-guns, the children scattered like sparrows. The aeroplane disappeared as quickly as it had come, but on the field some crumpled and lifeless bundles of bright clothing remained. The nature of the new war was already clear."

—*Polish officer Wladyslaw Anders*

GLOSSARY

ARTILLERY

Large guns or missile launchers, as distinguished from small arms; also, the troops or branch of the military that uses these weapons.

CARBINE

A firearm similar to a rifle but with a shorter barrel, making it easier to handle.

CASUALTY

A person who is injured, missing, or killed during a military campaign.

CONVOY

A group of ships or other vehicles traveling together for protection.

FISSION

The splitting of an atom to release energy.

INCENDIARY

A weapon used to start fires.

INFANTRY

A group of soldiers trained and armed to fight on foot.

INFRASTRUCTURE

The physical structures, such as roads, railways, and power plants, that make it possible for a city or nation to function.

MECHANIZED
Equipped with armored, tracked vehicles.

PILLBOX
An enclosed concrete structure used as a defensive outpost.

PROPAGANDA
Information that carries facts or details slanted to favor a single point of view or political bias.

PROPELLANT
The explosive material within a bullet that provides the forward force to fire the bullet.

RADIATION
A form of energy that can damage living tissue.

STRAFE
Attack from the air at close range by low-flying aircraft with machine guns or cannons.

TRENCH
A long, narrow hole dug in the ground by soldiers to give them cover from enemy fire.

ADDITIONAL RESOURCES

SELECTED BIBLIOGRAPHY

Hastings, Max. *Inferno: The World at War, 1939–1945*. New York: Vintage, 2011. Print.

The Illustrated Encyclopedia of Weapons of World War II. Ed. Chris Bishop. London: Amber, 2014. Print.

The Oxford Companion to World War II. Ed. I. C. B. Dear. Oxford: Oxford UP, 1995. Print.

FURTHER READINGS

Adams, Simon. *World War II*. New York: DK, 2014. Print.

Hamen, Susan E. *World War II*. Minneapolis, MN: Abdo, 2014. Print.

Hamilton, John. *World War II: Weapons*. Minneapolis, MN: Abdo, 2012. Print.

WEBSITES

To learn more about Essential Library of World War II, visit **booklinks.abdopublishing.com**. These links are routinely monitored and updated to provide the most current information available.

PLACES TO VISIT

National Museum of the US Air Force
1100 Spaatz Street
Dayton, OH 45431
937-255-3286
http://www.nationalmuseum.af.mil
The official museum of the US Air Force features hundreds of historical aircraft, including many from World War II. See the B-17, the B-29, the P-51, and other US aircraft from the war. Also included are many foreign planes, including the Bf 109, the Spitfire, and the Japanese Zero.

The Tank Museum
Linsay Road
Bovington, Dorset BH20 6JG
United Kingdom
+44 1929 405096
http://www.tankmuseum.org
This museum possesses the world's largest collection of historic tanks, including the major German and US types from World War II. Get an up-close view of Shermans, Tigers, Panthers, and many other models.

SOURCE NOTES

CHAPTER 1. WAGING A NEW WAR

1. "Stuka." *Encyclopædia Britannica*. Encyclopædia Britannica, 2015. Web. 21 Feb. 2015.

2. Max Hastings. *Inferno: The World at War, 1939–1945*. New York: Vintage, 2011. Print. 9.

3. *The Illustrated Encyclopedia of Weapons of World War II*. Ed. Chris Bishop. London: Amber, 2014. Print. 905.

4. *The Oxford Companion to World War II*. Ed. I. C. B. Dear. Oxford: Oxford UP, 1995. Print. 363.

5. Max Hastings. *Armageddon: The Battle for Germany, 1944–1945*. New York: Vintage, 2005. Print. 78.

6. *The Oxford Companion to World War II*. Ed. I. C. B. Dear. Oxford: Oxford UP, 1995. Print. 1183.

7. Ibid. 1216.

CHAPTER 2. SMALL ARMS

1. Geoffrey C. Ward and Ken Burns. *The War: An Intimate History, 1941–1945*. New York: Knopf, 2007. Print. 216.

2. *The Illustrated Encyclopedia of Weapons of World War II*. Ed. Chris Bishop. London: Amber, 2014. Print. 238.

3. A. J. Barker. *British and American Infantry Weapons of World War II*. London: Arms and Armor, 1969. Print. 28.

4. *The Illustrated Encyclopedia of Weapons of World War II*. Ed. Chris Bishop. London: Amber, 2014. Print. 246.

CHAPTER 3. HEAVY WEAPONS

1. *The Illustrated Encyclopedia of Weapons of World War II*. Ed. Chris Bishop. London: Amber, 2014. Print. 262.

2. Ibid. 268.

3. "The Battle for Iwo Jima." *The National WWII Museum*. The National WWII Museum, n.d. Web. 21 Feb. 2015.

4. *The Oxford Companion to World War II*. Ed. I. C. B. Dear. Oxford: Oxford UP, 1995. Print. 953.

5. *The Illustrated Encyclopedia of Weapons of World War II*. Ed. Chris Bishop. London: Amber, 2014. Print. 218.

6. Ibid. 222.

CHAPTER 4. LONG-RANGE DESTRUCTION

1. *The Oxford Companion to World War II*. Ed. I. C. B. Dear. Oxford: Oxford UP, 1995. Print. 57.

2. *The Illustrated Encyclopedia of Weapons of World War II*. Ed. Chris Bishop. London: Amber, 2014. Print. 130.

3. Max Hastings. *Inferno: The World at War, 1939–1945.* New York: Vintage, 2011. Print. 294.

4. Ibid.

5. *The Illustrated Encyclopedia of Weapons of World War II.* Ed. Chris Bishop. London: Amber, 2014. Print. 145.

6. Hickman Powell. "Two Guns for One." *Popular Science.* Nov. 1942. 54. *Google Book Search.* Web. 21 Feb. 2015.

7. *The Illustrated Encyclopedia of Weapons of World War II.* Ed. Chris Bishop. London: Amber, 2014. Print. 133.

8. Ibid. 134.

9. Ibid. 185.

10. Ibid.

CHAPTER 5. ROLLING ARMOR

1. *The Illustrated Encyclopedia of Weapons of World War II.* Ed. Chris Bishop. London: Amber, 2014. Print. 13–14.

2. Ibid. 14–15.

3. David Stone. *Hitler's Army: The Men, Machines, and Organization, 1939–1945.* Minneapolis: Zenith, 2009. Print. 174.

4. David E. Johnson. *Fast Tanks and Heavy Bombers: Innovation in the US Army, 1917–1945.* Ithaca: Cornell UP, 1998. Print. 189.

5. *The Illustrated Encyclopedia of Weapons of World War II.* Ed. Chris Bishop. London: Amber, 2014. Print. 11–41.

6. "Battle of Kursk." *Encyclopædia Britannica.* Encyclopædia Britannica, 2015. Web. 21 Feb. 2015.

7. Ibid.

8. Ibid.

9. George Forty. *Tank Warfare in the Second World War: An Oral History.* London: Constable, 1998. Print. 165.

CHAPTER 6. THE WAR AT SEA

1. *The Oxford Companion to World War II.* Ed. I. C. B. Dear. Oxford: Oxford UP, 1995. Print. 1199.

2. Ibid. 1083.

3. "U boats." *Encyclopædia Britannica.* Encyclopædia Britannica, 2015. Web. 21 Feb. 2015.

4. *The Oxford Companion to World War II.* Ed. I. C. B. Dear. Oxford: Oxford UP, 1995. Print. 43.

SOURCE NOTES
CONTINUED

5. Ibid. 1119.

6. "U boats." *Encyclopædia Britannica*. Encyclopædia Britannica, 2015. Web. 21 Feb. 2015.

7. *The Oxford Companion to World War II*. Ed. I. C. B. Dear. Oxford: Oxford UP, 1995. Print. 1082.

8. Max Hastings. *Retribution: The Battle for Japan, 1944–1945*. New York: Vintage, 2009. Print. 273.

9. Max Hastings. *Inferno: The World at War, 1939–1945*. New York: Vintage, 2011. Print. 629.

10. *The Illustrated Encyclopedia of Weapons of World War II*. Ed. Chris Bishop. London: Amber, 2014. Print. 525.

11. Ibid. 526.

12. Ibid.

13. Ibid.

CHAPTER 7. THE RISE OF CARRIERS

1. *The Illustrated Encyclopedia of Weapons of World War II*. Ed. Chris Bishop. London: Amber, 2014. Print. 515.

2. Ibid.

3. Ibid.

4. Ibid.

5. Ibid. 506.

6. Paul Kennedy. *Engineers of Victory: The Problem Solvers Who Turned the Tide in the Second World War*. New York: Random, 2013. Print. 320.

7. *The Illustrated Encyclopedia of Weapons of World War II*. Ed. Chris Bishop. London: Amber, 2014. Print. 427.

8. Ibid.

9. Ibid. 427.

10. Max Hastings. *Retribution: The Battle for Japan, 1944–1945*. New York: Vintage, 2009. Print. 108.

11. Ibid.

12. Ibid.

13. *The Oxford Companion to World War II*. Ed. I. C. B. Dear. Oxford: Oxford UP, 1995. Print. 944.

14. Ibid.

15. John Keegan. *The Second World War*. London: Hutchinson, 1989. Print. 278.

CHAPTER 8. WINNING THE SKY

1. Geoffrey C. Ward and Ken Burns. *The War: An Intimate History, 1941–1945*. New York: Knopf, 2007. Print. 84.

2. Ibid.

3. Ibid.

4. *The Oxford Companion to World War II*. Ed. I. C. B. Dear. Oxford: Oxford UP, 1995. Print. 22.

5. "Spitfire." *Encyclopædia Britannica*. Encyclopædia Britannica, 2015. Web. 21 Feb. 2015.

6. *The Illustrated Encyclopedia of Weapons of World War II*. Ed. Chris Bishop. London: Amber, 2014. Print. 303.

7. Ibid. 321.

8. Geoffrey C. Ward and Ken Burns. *The War: An Intimate History, 1941–1945*. New York: Knopf, 2007. Print. 117.

9. Ibid. 120.

10. *The Oxford Companion to World War II*. Ed. I. C. B. Dear. Oxford: Oxford UP, 1995. Print. 149.

11. Ibid.

12. *The Illustrated Encyclopedia of Weapons of World War II*. Ed. Chris Bishop. London: Amber, 2014. Print. 149.

13. "Firebombing of Tokyo." *History*. A&E Television Networks, n.d. Web. 21 Feb. 2015.

14. Max Hastings. *Inferno: The World at War, 1939–1945*. New York: Vintage, 2011. Print. 628.

15. "The Few." *The Churchill Centre*. Churchill Centre, n.d. Web. 21 Feb. 2015.

CHAPTER 9. A BLOODY END

1. Max Hastings. *Inferno: The World at War, 1939–1945*. New York: Vintage, 2011. Print. 622.

2. Ibid.

3. Max Hastings. *Retribution: The Battle for Japan, 1944–1945*. New York: Vintage, 2009. Print. 167.

4. "Japan's Secret WWII Weapon: Balloon Bombs." *National Geographic*. National Geographic Society, n.d. Web. 21 Feb. 2015.

5. *The Oxford Companion to World War II*. Ed. I. C. B. Dear. Oxford: Oxford UP, 1995. Print. 1249.

6. Ibid. 1252.

7. "Fact File: Hiroshima and Nagasaki." *WW2 People's War*. BBC, 15 Oct. 2014. Web. 21 Feb. 2015.

INDEX

ABOUT THE AUTHOR

Arnold Ringstad has written more than 30 books for audiences ranging from kindergarteners to high-schoolers. He has also published research in the *Journal of Cold War Studies*. He is an avid reader of books about history and space exploration. Ringstad graduated from the University of Minnesota in 2011. He resides in Minnesota.

ABOUT THE CONSULTANT

James D. Scudieri has a PhD from the Graduate School and University Center, CUNY, with a major in military history and a minor in British history. Scudieri served 30 years on active duty as a US Army logistician, with assignments in the United States, Korea, Germany, Afghanistan, and Iraq. He completed four years as an instructor in the Department of History, United States Military Academy of West Point in New York. Scudieri finished five years as an instructor in the Department of Military Strategy, Plans, and Operations at the US Army War College, a year as Deputy Dean, and most recently as a civilian professor of theater planning. He is currently an independent consultant and research analyst at the Army Heritage and Education Center in the Historical Services Division.